BestDressed

BestDressed

Fashion from the Birth of Couture to Today

Dilys E. Blum and H. Kristina Haugland

Photography by Lynn Rosenthal and Graydon Wood

Philadelphia Museum of Art

This book is published on the occasion of the exhibition
Best Dressed: 250 Years of Style
Philadelphia Museum of Art
October 21, 1997, to January 4, 1998

Cover: Detail of Court Presentation Ensemble, 1950, designed by Norman
Hartnell (pp. 48–49)
Title page: Detail of Two-Piece Evening Dress, 1979, designed by Zandra
Rhodes (pp. 62–63)

This publication and the exhibition would not have been possible without the
volunteers and interns in the Department of Costume and Textiles who enthusi-
astically and generously helped with everything from petticoats to paper hair:
Robert Balicki, Nancy Bergman, Misha Brooker, Millicent Bvunzawabaya, Lauren
Chang, Andrea Dade, Barbara Darlin, Nancy Fawley, Anne Goldstein, Rebecca
Hellrich, Valerie Kontes-Baron, Catherine Lucey, Dean Ockert, Julie Panebianco,
Gabrielle Revlock, Anne Rogers, Rachel Rosenbaum, Hillary Sculthorpe, Timothy
Sibley, Lori Spector, Stacy Sweet, Dana Tepper, Gayla Weng, and Elizabeth Wells

Produced by the Department of Publications and Graphics
Philadelphia Museum of Art
Benjamin Franklin Parkway at 26th Street
P.O. Box 7646
Philadelphia, PA 19101-7646

Edited by George H. Marcus and Curtis R. Scott
Design and art direction by Alex Castro, Castro/Arts, Baltimore
Color separations and printing by Amilcare Pizzi, S.p.A., Milan

Library of Congress Cataloging-in-Publication Data

Blum, Dilys E., 1947–
        Best dressed : fashion from the birth of couture to today / Dilys E.
Blum and H. Kristina Haugland ; photography by Lynn Rosenthal and
Graydon Wood.
            p.   cm.
        "Published on the occasion of the exhibition . . . at the
Philadelphia Museum of Art from October 21, 1997 to January 4,
1998"--T.p. verso.
            ISBN 0-87633-118-5 (alk. paper)
        1. Costume design--History--20th century--Exhibitions. 2. Costume
design--History--19th century--Exhibitions. 3. Costume design-
-History--20th century--Pictorial works--Exhibitions. 4. Costume
design--History--19th century--Pictorial works--Exhibitions.
5. Fashion designers--History--20th century--Exhibitions.
6. Fashion designers--History--19th century--Exhibitions.
7. Philadelphia Museum of Art--Exhibitions. I. Haugland, H. Kristina,
1959- . II. Philadelphia Museum of Art.
III. Title.
TT 507.B58 1997   97-31268
746.9'2'074748211--dc21   CIP

Preface

The complex effort involved in the creation of a major exhibition drawn from the rich holdings of the Department of Costume and Textiles at the Philadelphia Museum of Art has borne many fruits, including a beautifully illustrated handbook of its textiles, which has just been published. It has also inspired the present publication, not a comprehensive catalogue but a dazzling tour of selected highlights from the museum's collection of fashionable dresses beginning with several masterpieces by the father of *haute couture,* Charles Frederick Worth, most of which were made for and owned (or yearned after) by American women, many of them Philadelphians. The first garments collected by the museum after its founding in 1876 provided early costume historians with a rich resource for the study of historic American dress, and with the opening of the first costume galleries under the sponsorship of the Fashion Group of Philadelphia in 1947, the collection expanded its focus to include fine examples of contemporary design as well.

This exhibition, the first in twenty years to survey the costume collection, ranges far afield to touch upon many strengths, from Asia to Europe to North America, and from the mid-eighteenth century to the present. Launched with the invaluable support of a grant from the National Endowment for the Arts, which has done so much to assist American art museums in their central mission of cataloguing, publishing, and displaying their collections, the exhibition and its related publications have in turn depended on the individual generosity and hard work of many donors, museum staff, and volunteers, especially within the Department of Costume and Textiles. The support of the Fashion Group of Philadelphia has been unfailing over many years, and a succession of Crystal Balls raised funds that were essential to realizing the exhibition. Our warm appreciation goes particularly to Thomas Neil Crater, whose exuberant expertise did so much to ensure that the exhibition would encompass fine contemporary fashion, and we are grateful to Waring Hopkins, who offered invaluable assistance with new acquisitions. We owe special thanks to Maxine Lewis, chairman of the museum's committee on costume and textiles, whose enthusiasm for this project since its inception has translated so directly into help of every kind.

In the creation of the exhibition, the masterful installation design of Dextra Frankel set the stage for a brilliant variety of dress, while Lynn Rosenthal's and Graydon Wood's splendid photographs and Alex Castro's elegant design perform the same task for this book. The ideal mix of flair, careful treatment, and attention to detail on the part of H. Kristina Haugland, assistant curator of costume and textiles, Monica Brown, departmental assistant, and Sara Reiter, conservator, has brought back to life the dresses that enliven these pages and grace the exhibition galleries.

Above all, we are indebted to the formidable talents of generations of both anonymous craftsmen and celebrated designers who created these astonishing garments and to the many generous donors who have graciously shared them with the public.

Anne d'Harnoncourt
The George D. Widener Director

Dilys E. Blum
Curator, Costume and Textiles

Haute Couture

Charles Frederick Worth became the dominant figure of French fashion during the early 1860s, transforming the craft of dressmaking into the art of *haute couture*. With his unflagging invention, experimentation with construction techniques, and genius for self-promotion, he laid the foundations for the next century of high fashion. In the traditionally feminine field of fashion, the success of a man—and an Englishman at that—was unprecedented and somewhat scandalous. Nevertheless, the firm that Worth had founded with his Swedish business partner Otto Gustaf Bobergh gained the patronage of the French empress Eugénie as well as the right to use the imperial coat of arms on its label. In this charming evening dress from about 1870, Worth utilized only one fabric, a shimmering satin beautifully suited to the full, back-gathered skirt that characterized fashion's transition from hoop to bustle. Its graceful train is edged with rows of self ruffles, which inspired by eighteenth-century styles, are also applied up each side to give the appearance of an overskirt open to show off three tiers of fabric swags. Sparingly finished with tulle and lace, the dress exemplifies Worth's renowned ability to create "simple" styles as well as the extravagant apparel that suited this era of excess.

Arbiter of Style

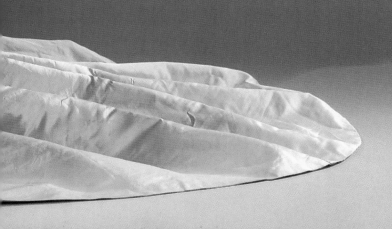

Worth created for himself the role of arbiter of style: he no longer merely furnished fashions, he dictated them. Rather than design each dress in collaboration with a client, he introduced twice-yearly collections with live mannequins wearing model dresses. These designs were then adapted to suit each individual customer so that Worth's clothing always gave the impression of being the unique creation of his artistic genius. His business, however, was run almost as an assembly line; by 1870, the year his partnership ended, his Paris fashion house at 7, rue de la Paix, employed twelve hundred seamstresses to produce hundreds of new garments every week. Prevailing taste at this time preferred rich contrasting harmonies of color and combinations of diverse textures. This complex bustle skirt of olive green silk faille draped asymmetrically over a shimmering trained underskirt of chartreuse satin also features maroon velvet supporting faille bows up one side and accents of brilliant foliage appliqué. The ensemble has two bodices: this sleeved one with a low, square neckline, suitable for afternoon or dinner wear, and a sleeveless, décolleté bodice for formal evenings.

Paris à la Mode

When visiting Paris, many wealthy women made it their mission to fill their trunks with the latest styles. Their time was happily spent going to the numerous required fittings, confident that a Parisian wardrobe would have that *je ne sais quoi* that was both untranslatable and inimitable. While many followed the well-traveled path to Worth's door, others of a more adventurous spirit sought out the craftsmanship and creativity of the city's other distinguished *maisons de couture*. One of the couturiers especially favored by Americans was Emile Pingat, another male designer in competition with Worth. In this day dress, designed about 1876, Pingat makes effective use of a bold striped fabric: caught up in front drapery and then cascading down the bustled back, it also sparingly accents the bodice at the collar and cuffs and at the sides of the back. The stripes are skillfully utilized again, on the diagonal, in loops finishing the train, and the motif is echoed by variegated fringe edging the embroidered net trim. Pingat's eye for detail and his flawless workmanship are evident even in the understated areas of his design, as in the vertical tucks that subtly accentuate the fit of the solid blue back of the bodice.

REVUE DE LA MODE

Export Wear

THE HOUSE OF WORTH continued to dominate fashion in the 1880s, catering to a large international clientele who understood and coveted the cachet of a Worth gown. With his name a household word, Charles Frederick Worth was known not only by those who could patronize his Paris *maison*—and pay the extravagant sums he charged—but also by those who bought the models he exported across the world. This opulent brocade evening dress belonged to an American, Mrs. Ernest Fenollosa, wife of an eminent professor and art historian, who lived in Tokyo for twelve years. Mrs. Fenollosa probably purchased the gown on a trip to Paris in 1887, and it is obvious that, like many other women of the time, she greatly prized a garment from Worth. She owned another dress, of white and gold silk brocade, that is identical in cut to this one but without a label, indicating that she may have had a dressmaker copy her Worth creation line for line. Such was the fame of Worth that, with the new openness of Japan to Western culture, his gowns were even ordered for the empress herself.

The Cult of Chiffon

In her 1902 book *The Cult of Chiffon*, Mrs. Eric Pritchard recommended that a wise woman clothe herself in lovely raiment, "displaying in her very faintly perfumed *frou-frouing* draperies that delicious coquetry which no woman can afford to disdain, and which is and ever has been her greatest charm, and her greatest power." With their flowing lines and extremely feminine style, tea gowns were the essence of this Edwardian ideal. Worn for informal early evening entertaining, they were often made of chiffon, and were extolled by Mrs. Pritchard as "the garment of illusion, poetry, and mystic grace." This tea gown, created about 1905 by the Parisian house of Jeanne Hallée, which was run by two former Worth employees, comprises a gown and a sleeveless tunic. The gown, made over a boned underbodice, is of silk chiffon over silk satin and is luxuriously trimmed with self ruffles and lace. The diaphanous tunic, bordered down the front by ribbon run through ruching and decorated by ribbon bows, is further embellished with a latticework of lace and delicate fly fringe, and like the dress, is finished with bouquets of ribbon flowers with pendulous buds.

New York Finery

This majestic gown by Mrs. Dunstan, one of New York's many fine dress-makers at the turn of the century, was made to suit the ideal woman of the period: mature and self-assured, with a rounded figure and a commanding bosom thrust forward. Married women were especially favored by fashion at the time, since the most elaborate gowns were reserved for them. As Mrs. Frank Learned noted in *The Etiquette of New York To-day* (1906), at dinners, balls, and evening parties, and in their boxes at the opera, young women were deemed appropriately dressed only in modest necklines and "no jewelled ornaments . . . except, perhaps, a string of pearls"; matrons, however, in low-necked gowns, wore "handsome satins, velvets, crêpes or spangled nets"—as well as their finest jewels. Two contrasting types of decoration on this ivory satin creation exemplify the Edwardian love of intricate—and expensive—surface treatment, which required vast amounts of delicate hand-work. The neckline and the tulle at the bottom of the skirt are embellished with organic, Art Nouveau decoration embroidered in gilt threads lavishly bedecked with rhinestones, while geometric motifs fan out from the slim waist; layers of silk tulle are applied and outlined in different types of embroidery, then further accented with metallic thread, rhinestones, and sequins in graduated sizes.

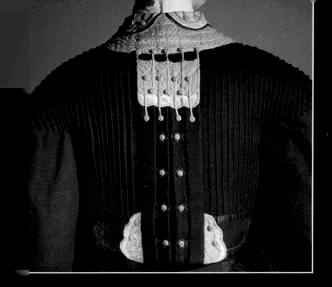

DURING THE FIRST DECADE of the twentieth century, many of Europe's progressive architects designed interiors that were conceived as total works of art, leading them to consider the relationships between architecture, design, and fashion. At the same time, the dress reform movement sought to rationalize women's clothing by making it more comfortable, more natural, and more aesthetically pleasing. The Belgian Henry van de Velde was one of a number of well-known architects who advocated clothing and jewelry designs that both integrated women into their surroundings and adhered to reformist ideals. While the Art Nouveau style is reflected in the design of the label of this winter walking outfit, made about 1905 by the Brussels fashion house Furst, its strongly contrasting palette of navy, ocher, and cream and its straight lines and geometric embroidered decoration reveal the influence of Van de Velde's geometric designs as well as those of the Vienna Secessionist Josef Hoffmann, who was also active in Brussels at this time.

Reforming Fashion

One of the services offered by American department stores was custom dressmaking, which often included making up garments copied from French designs. Each spring and fall the store's buyers or agents would purchase models and designs in Paris; with each purchase came a memorandum indicating the source for the model's fabric and the yardage required for the gown. These Paris models were usually presented to special customers in separate departments, like Wanamaker's Little Gray Salons, that were decorated to replicate the experience a woman might have shopping at one of the exclusive dressmaking establishments on the place

Elegant Emporiums

Vendôme or the rue de la Paix in Paris. These two outfits were both custom-made by department stores. The chiffon dinner dress, dating to about 1912, came from B. Altman in New York and has the word "Paris" on its label, emphasizing the fact that it was based on a French model. Paris, however, was not the only source for designs; London, Berlin, and Vienna were known for their tailor-made clothes, especially riding habits and walking outfits, such as this cream wool ensemble fashionably trimmed with machine-made Irish lace, which was purchased about 1904 from Gimbel Brothers in Philadelphia.

DREAM DRESSES

Described by the press as "the first English lady of title . . . to dress the Four Hundred," the English couturiere Lady Duff Gordon, known as Lucile, opened a New York branch of her famous London dressmaking business in 1910, expanding to Paris in 1912 and Chicago in 1915. Lucile aimed to make an art of beautiful dressing, and her "Dream Dresses" were fairy-tale creations of shimmering silks, gossamer laces, and delicate rainbows of ribbon. Influenced by her early designs for lingerie and tea gowns, Lucile's dresses, which she also referred to as "Gowns of Emotion," were given suitably romantic names. This pale aqua dinner dress, entitled "Happiness," is from her Fall 1916 New York collection and represents the quintessential Lucile creation. It was designed in the eighteenth-century style she often favored, its hooped skirt drawn back to reveal a delicate silk, lace, and ribbon petticoat.

Portrait of Fashion

The New York designer Harry Collins, billed as a "Creator of Art in Dress," designed this gown for the Long Island art collector and socialite Mabel Brady Garvan, who wore it in 1921 when she sat for her portrait, shown surrounded by her four well-dressed children. The artist, Philip de László, among the most fashionable portrait painters of the period, freely interpreted the details of the garment but succeeded in capturing the essence of its style. Combining elements of evening dress, at-home wear, and fancy dress, the gown features a picturesque short bodice of figured lamé decorated with colorful festooned bands and a fanciful bouquet. The newly stylish shortened skirt is made more dignified and dramatic by a long sheer overskirt ending in a train; it is given further elegance by the georgette drapery that loops around the body and then sweeps gracefully over the arm.

EGYPTOMANIA

WITH THE DISCOVERY IN 1922
of the tomb of the ancient Egyptian
pharaoh Tutankhamen, "Tutmania"
gripped the public, and many dress designers introduced novel Egyptian color
schemes and decoration into their collections. Paul Poiret, the most famous designer during the years immediately before
World War I, employed bold, embroidered
"hieroglyphic" motifs in this striking dress
from late in his career. The accompanying
hat, which follows the shape of Egyptian
hairstyles, sports the contrasting stripes
characteristic of pharaonic art. Even the
Parisian designer Gustave Beer, known for
his "conservative elegance for conservative
patrons," was caught up in the fad,
although the ensemble he designed makes
more subtle use of inspiration from Egypt.
His sober wool faille dress and jacket,
trimmed with fluted bands of self material,
are enlivened by bands of turquoise silk
embroidery and contrasting squares of
dark fabric and pink beading. Set within
embroidered cartouche-like rectangles on
the jacket and belt are painted metal
medallions in the form of scarabs, the
beetles that symbolized the sun god
to the ancient Egyptians.

Renaissance Romance

Wedding gowns were a particular specialty of Jeanne Lanvin, who began her career as a milliner and presided over a couture house also known for its children's dresses and mother-daughter ensembles. Lanvin's fashions often drew on the past, and she frequently used her own extensive collection of historic costume, costume books, and fashion plates for inspiration. This wedding ensemble, designed by Lanvin in 1925, evokes the feeling of early fifteenth-century Italian fashion; its silver lamé appliqué and embroidered feather design as well as its rounded bridal headdress recall Pisanello's well-known studies of Northern Italian women wearing gowns with winged, capelike sleeves and oversized turbans.

THE PHILADELPHIA SEASON

The sisters Elizabeth and Ann Stetson, granddaughters of the founder of the Stetson hat company, wore these matching dresses in 1927 at Ann's coming-out tea party at "Idro," the family's house in Elkins Park, near Philadelphia. Pretty frocks such as these, made of net or gauze in white or delicate pastel tints to suggest youth and innocence, were the appropriate wear for young women making their social debuts. Given the name "La Belle Rose," the dresses were created by Madame Meeley at her workrooms at 2012 Walnut Street in Philadelphia. They were made in contrasting colors for the two sisters, who liked to dress alike: the pink of the showroom model was chosen by Ann, age eighteen, while Elizabeth, age twenty, selected aqua. To highlight the charms of the two young women, the crossover bodices are simply knotted at the shoulders, and the full, *robes de style* skirts, supported by boned understructures at the sides, are covered with rows of tulle ruffles. These shorten and overlap in front and gracefully reveal the lace hems of delicate matching satin slips.

In Full Bloom

DELLA THOMPSON LUTES noted in her 1923 etiquette book *The Gracious Hostess* that well-dressed women should harmonize with their surroundings, choosing their apparel to suit the overall picture produced by each social occasion. At garden parties, where colorful flowers are enhanced by the green of leaves, trees, and hedges, women should don "bright pretty dresses and gay nodding hats that are themselves like flowers" to be set off against the background of somber male attire. Dresses for summer garden parties or formal social events such as race meetings called for ethereal creations that were light, cool, and colorful. Even at a time when the fashionable ideal was a boyish form and the elimination of decorative excess, women's wardrobes retained some garments that utilized frankly feminine fabrics and patterns. The skilled, unknown dressmakers who created these two summer frocks made elegant use of floral motifs: flowers from the bright, printed chiffon are used as appliqués around the circular collar that creates its fluttering sleeves, while small, sprightly bouquets are painstakingly beaded onto the solid navy chiffon.

PAST INTO PRESENT

The creations of Mariano Fortuny are endowed with a magical presence, and his textile designs and the cut of his garments span both time and geography. Renaissance Italy and the Middle and Far East provided models for many of his garments as well as for his luxurious velvets stenciled with metallic pigments. Classical Greek dress inspired his most popular design, the finely pleated silk "Delphos" gown, which the French novelist Marcel Proust described in *A Remembrance of Things Past* as "faithfully antique but forcefully original." Produced from about 1907 until his death in 1949, it was originally intended to be worn at home for entertaining, but by the end of World War I had become acceptable evening wear on other occasions. It was often worn with a velvet jacket or three-quarter-length coat such as this one, which derives in its fabric and style from a seventeenth-century Persian example. The velvet-paneled long gown, another of Fortuny's popular creations, is stenciled with what was described as a Moorish design; it has his signature silk pleats inset at the sides and sleeves, held in place with cords looped over glass beads from the island of Murano, near Venice, the Spanish designer's adopted city.

STREAMLINING STYLE

THE STREAMLINED SILHOUETTE of the 1930s mirrored the aesthetics of the Machine Age, and the words used to describe its art and architecture—precision, simplicity, and smoothness—can also be applied to the period's fashions. Precision cutting and seaming, economy of line, and the use of shimmering satins and velvets were hallmarks of its dress design, which helped to transform the body into a simple classical column, a reflection of the Platonic ideal that formed the basis of its design philosophy. This shell pink evening gown was designed by Augustabernard, who dressed chic Paris during the late 1920s and early 1930s and also found enthusiastic clients among New York's custom dressmakers and import houses, among them Henri Bendel, Bergdorf Goodman, and Thurn, from whom it was purchased. Like many Augustabernard designs, the gown glides over the body and is unadorned except for its deeply cut back of rich magenta velvet, which ties into a bow over flowing panels of satin held in place with shirring, a characteristic Augustabernard detail. The gown was captured for *Vogue* in 1933 by the noted photographer George Hoyningen-Huene.

Shocking

Called "the dressmaker of eccentricity" by the French author Jean Cocteau, Elsa Schiaparelli is best remembered today for her chic, witty fashions, which took Paris by storm in the 1930s. Her designs were sometimes startling and often "shocking," a word she herself coined for the cyclamen pink color that became her trademark and is seen here on the brilliant sunburst buttons of the deep purple velvet jacket. One of her most successful and enduring creations was the dinner suit, ubiquitous during the 1930s, which combined an exquisitely embroidered evening jacket, such as these from her Winter 1937–38 collection, with a plain, figure-hugging, backless sheath or a long skirt. Her collaboration with the finest craftsmen resulted in fashions that are indisputably works of art, with embroideries such as these by the renowned firm of Lesage and buttons by Jean Clément, the genius behind Schiaparelli's many inventive accessories.

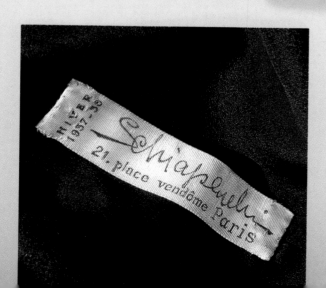

In 1938 Elsa Schiaparelli dressed Mae West for the film *Every Day's a Holiday*. The curvaceous actress became the inspiration not only for Schiaparelli's most famous perfume bottle, designed by Leonor Fini in the form of a dress-maker's dummy, but also for the extravagantly draped bustle dresses in her 1939 collections. Bustle dresses appeared with many different fabrics, from Gay '90s prints designed by the artists Christian Bérard and Marcel Vertès to the colorful stripes seen here, which appeared in *Vogue* that year in a charming sketch by Bérard.

BACK TO BUSTLES

HOLLYWOOD CLASSICS

WITH HOLLYWOOD the glamour capital of the world, costume designers Adrian and Irene influenced fashion far beyond the confines of the silver screen. Adrian was head designer for Metro-Goldwyn-Mayer from 1930 until 1942, when he established his ready-to-wear and custom clothing salon in Beverly Hills. In the early 1930s he introduced the broad-shouldered, slim-hipped look that became the fashionable shape during World War II. His intricately perfected cut is evident in this green and brown twill suit from 1947. The diagonal of the fabric is complemented by the jacket's front seaming and is repeated in diagonal, welted pockets, while the curved seam on the chest is mirrored in the collar and repeated by the hanging over-sleeves. Irene, who was head of the custom department at Bullocks Wilshire during the 1930s, followed Adrian as head designer at MGM, where she too dressed the studio's stars, including Joan Crawford. She also opened a wholesale ready-to-wear business in 1947 and was the first important costume designer to have boutiques in department stores throughout the United States. Her tan and mocha striped suit, sold by Nan Duskin of Philadelphia, demonstrates her masterful manipulation of geometric-patterned wool in slim yet not severe suits.

Credited by no less an authority than fellow couturier Cristóbal Balenciaga with raising dressmaking from an applied art to a pure art form, Charles James was the *enfant terrible* of fashion in the late 1940s and 1950s. Self-taught, he was a perfectionist who obsessed over the cut and construction of each garment, producing designs that were completely idiosyncratic. James's virtuoso ball gowns were engineered to be sublime sartorial sculptures and were usually fashioned of lustrous heavy silk satin that forgave no mistakes in either pattern or stitching. Nevertheless, the shaping was so calculated that James's garments often integrated features that were extraneous in less analytical clothing. The bow at the back of the pink gown is not applied; rather, it is cut in one with the skirt front and thus becomes integral with it. The silhouettes of his evening gowns often featured full, intricately shaped skirts over elaborate understructures, such as the horsehair interlining that supports the sides of the skirt of the yellow gown. The luxurious elegance of James's satin ball gowns was captured in 1948 in this photographic tableau by Cecil Beaton.

Sculpted in Satin

Dior by Day

Christian Dior brought femininity, grace, and elegance to postwar fashion. In his first collection from 1947, which the editor of *Harper's Bazaar* christened the "New Look," Dior redefined the fashionable silhouette: short skirts, limited in width and length by French wartime restrictions, were replaced by long skirts using yards of fabric; square shoulders gave way to a more natural, rounded look; and nipped-in waists emphasized hips made fuller by pleats or padding, adding a new voluptuousness to the female form. The tailored wool suit, called "Avenue Hoche," from Dior's Spring/Summer 1949 "Trompe l'Oeil" or "Illusion" collection, further develops the design principles of the New Look. Strategically placed pockets emphasize the hips and diminish the waist, while the swing-pleated panel at the back of the skirt adds movement to the silhouette without adding fullness. In contrast, the two-piece dress from Dior's Fall 1952 "Profile" collection, dramatically silhouetted in black (Dior's favorite color at that moment), creates a sharper, more defined line. Its stark simplicity is relieved only by the keyhole neck and the buttons, which emphasize the hips and sloping shoulders.

NORMAN HARTNELL designed theater costumes when he was a student at Cambridge, and throughout his long career he favored theatrical clothes perfectly suited to grand occasions. The preeminent British designer of his time, he was appointed dressmaker to the royal family in 1938; his flatteringly feminine designs, often modeled after the crinolined gowns of the mid-nineteenth century, set royal style for decades. In 1947 he designed the wedding dress of Princess Elizabeth, and in 1953, her coronation gown. This lavish dress, designed for an evening court presentation, exemplifies Hartnell's gala style, with jeweled encrustations of flowers above a full skirt made of yards and yards of tulle over sparkling gold lamé. It was completed with a court headdress of Prince of Wales feathers and a train that hangs from the shoulders, and accompanied by a feather fan, all traditionally worn by a woman when formally presented to the monarch. The ensemble, the highlight of a "Command Performance" showing of British fashions at Philadelphia's Bellevue-Stratford Hotel in 1950, is one of the last of its kind, since formal evening court presentations, discontinued during the war, were not resumed.

Presented at Court

The Essence of Spain

The designs of the Spanish-born couturier
Cristóbal Balenciaga were simple yet
dramatic, perfect in detail, and exquisitely shaped. He frequently drew on his
Spanish heritage to create fashions that
were inspired both by the works of Spain's
greatest painters, such as Velázquez,
Goya, and Zurbarán, and by the regional
dress of its people. The costume of the
flamenco dancer, with its flounced skirt
cut short in front and dipping down in
the back, was the source for this dramatic
evening dress from Balenciaga's Spring
1951 collection. In his version, a strapless
black silk organza evening dress is topped
with a removable, softly tailored, full-
length white cotton piqué overdress,
which is cut away to reveal a cascade
of feathered organza petals.

casually chic

During the years after World War II, the Italian designer Emilio Pucci revolutionized sportswear, turning casual into chic. His name and that of Capri, the fashionable resort off the coast of Naples, became synonymous with a relaxed style of dressing especially suited for the beach resorts frequented by the jet set during the 1950s. This ensemble, worn by Lauren Bacall, is typical of the Capri look. It includes slim, figure-hugging pants in finely woven cotton tapering to a few inches above the ankle, short shorts (not shown), a bikini top, and a tailored, square-cut, long-sleeved shirt. The shirt was worn loose by day but by night was provocatively unbuttoned, knotted at the waist, and accessorized with gold chains and jeweled sandals. The ensemble is from Pucci's "Siciliana" collection of Fall/Winter 1955–56, and its fabric, inspired by Italian sources like so many others he used during the period, derives from the Byzantine mosaic decorations of the cathedral of Monreale. In contrast, Claire McCardell's sportswear designs were simple, practical, and affordable, perfectly suited to the busy lives of American women. She is credited with many fashion "firsts" that have since become standard features of American sportswear. These include borrowing elements from work clothes, such as the brass tab closures she called "workclothes grippers," which fasten down the front of this sleeved wool knit bathing dress from 1953.

A Measure of Perfection

The garments created by James Galanos for his ready-to-wear fashion house in Los Angeles rival the best of *haute couture*. The quality of construction and painstaking attention to detail both inside and out speak to the skill of his workrooms as well as the designer's own perfectionism. From multilayered chiffon skirts—some made with fifty yards of cloth—to distinctive hand beading, such masterful handling of fabric is the essence of the Galanos style. The perfectly matched tartan plaid of this body-hugging evening dress from 1957 was beaded onto fine bias-cut cotton by the Los Angeles firm D. Getson Eastern Embroidery, which executes most of the designer's embroideries. It illustrates the complexity and beauty of Galanos's beaded fabrics, built up in layers with bugle beads and sequins to create the texture that is a distinctive feature of the designer's style.

The Total Look

Rudi Gernreich helped free women from the body-restraining clothing that was fashionable during the 1950s and 1960s. Refusing to follow the lead of French designers, he earned a reputation as the most original and radical designer in the United States. That reputation was cemented in his Fall 1964 collection with his introduction of the topless swimsuit, which he regarded not as a gratuitous display of the female body but as a sociological statement about freedom. This ensemble from the same collection—Gernreich's favorite—shows many of the designer's hallmarks. His simple, pared-down designs in malleable materials, such as this striped wool knit, reflect the influence of the leotards and tights worn by dancers, and his early career as a modern dancer is also evident in a concern for freedom of movement and how clothes look in motion. Gernreich treated the dress as simply one part of the picture, and put an emphasis on the integration of accessories, such as the striking legwear of this ensemble. The total look that resulted from Gernreich's view of modern clothing as an attitude, not a silhouette, was at once functional and comfortable, cerebral and graphic.

Paco Rabanne considered himself an artisan, not a couturier. He relied on the new technologies of the 1960s to provide innovative, offbeat materials and to make the common elements of garment construction, such as seams and fasteners, obsolete. In this dress with a low-cut back and knee-high front slit, metal rings link hundreds of silver and black plastic disks to create a mesh that is so revealing that it was usually worn over a body stocking. The dress comes from Rabanne's first collection in 1966, which he titled "Twelve Unwearable Dresses in Contemporary Materials." In contrast, Halston, who by the 1970s had become the supreme American fashion designer, created unconstricted, pared-down yet elegant clothes that were traditional, radically simple, and eminently wearable. Halston's penchant for vibrant colors and his conceptual use of fluid matte jersey are shown in this asymmetrical dress that wraps around itself and extends to form a draped sleeve.

Hardwear
and
Softwear

The Master's Touch

NORMAN NORELL worked in the French couture tradition, bringing the highest standards of design and workmanship— the finest fabrics, hand stitching, and exclusivity—to American ready-to-wear. Throughout his long career Norell refined and redefined the same basic designs to create classic, timeless clothes, such as this afternoon dress and jacket. Dating from 1968, it includes many Norell signatures: meticulous workmanship, a simple and elegant silhouette, the drama of black against a clear bright color, the pussycat bow, and a shirtwaist dress, here in black silk taffeta, its lavish full skirt set off by a wide patent leather belt.

Fantasy and Fashion

Zandra Rhodes is one of today's most creative and original designers. Her work is instantly recognizable, taking as its starting point her uniquely personal textile designs, which in turn influence the shape of her garments. A trip to China in 1979 inspired both the fabric and the form of this two-piece evening dress. The printed fabric design, which Rhodes called "Chinese Squares," is based on the trellises and fretwork that she saw during her travels, but these ornamental figures are com-plemented by the designer's own "scribble heads," images that recur in her other textiles. This dress, like all the clothing designs created for the same collection, was based on the dramatic robes worn in the tradi-tional Chinese ballet. Its pagoda sleeves are created from squares of the print, and each corner is weighted down with shimmering glass beads.

DAY INTO NIGHT

The classically elegant designs of Bill Blass are studies in contrasts and contradictions. His day clothes are impeccably cut in fabrics associated with the finest menswear—camelhair, tweeds, and flannels—and are often teamed in unexpected combinations of patterns and textures, such as two different plaids or satin paired with cashmere. For evening, his signature look is pure glamour and romance, a luxurious mix of sequins, satins, and embroidery. Here, however, Blass has turned the tables, and day becomes night: a bold black-and-white wool houndstooth plaid usually associated with daytime sportswear is transformed into a short, sexy, strapless dress for the evening.

ARCHITECT
OF
FASHION

Although Pierre Cardin's empire now extends from ready-to-wear to home furnishings to Maxim's restaurants, his *haute couture* collection continues to provide the designer with a laboratory in which to explore his creativity. Cardin is a master at manipulating fabric into dramatic architectonic forms. In the 1960s he used hard-edged bonded synthetics for geometric minimalist designs with a futuristic look; during the 1970s single layers of angora wool jersey were draped and pleated into fluid forms that flowed over the body; and in the 1980s fabric emphatically structured into flat planes for day clothes was complemented by crisp taffeta formed into extravagant flounces and ruffles for evening wear. In this short evening dress from 1987, an enormous, softly pleated taffeta ruffle, laid asymmetrically across body-hugging drapery, dramatically frames the face and fans out at one shoulder into a wing, which conceals an oversized organza flower.

Christian Lacroix is a master at
fantasy dressing, and his work can
be at once theatrical, decorative,
and unabashedly romantic. This
short evening dress is from the
designer's first "Luxe" collection,
Spring/Summer 1988, which had
flowers as its theme. It reveals
Lacroix's love affair with English
gardens and
particularly
his fascination

Hearts and Flowers

with roses, which he scattered full-
blown across the printed cotton
of this peplum-waisted dress. Silk
rosebuds, which Lacroix claims are
almost more intoxicating than real
ones, decorate the frilled-edged
"candy box" heart that forms the
strapless bodice of the dress,
its silhouette reminiscent of
eighteenth-century fashions
with their panniered skirts and
decorative stomachers.

CONCEPT CLOTHES

Issey Miyake transcends both his
Japanese heritage and his training in Western
couture to redefine the concept of clothing and
reinvent the activity of wearing clothes. With the
"Flying Saucer" dress of 1994, he shows how
modern clothes can be high-tech as
well as fun, uniting the advanced
technology of permanently pleated
polyester with the traditional form of paper
lanterns sold at Japanese fairs. While the dress
becomes an extension of the wearer, taking its
shape from the body beneath, its eccentric
silhouette is due to the nature of the fabric and
the seamed construction of the garment. The
dress, which simply pulls on, returns to its preset shape
after wearing and washing, and is easily stored in its
collapsed, accordion-pleated form. Yet this same dress is
also ever changing; its shape reacts to movement, and
both the creases of the fabric and the deeper structural
peaks and indentations catch every play of light,
creating an energetic and exuberant mood that is
reiterated in its festive bands of color.

REVEALING FORMS

Geoffrey Beene's clothing designs range from the simply elegant to the demurely feminine to the subtly witty, yet they are united within the designer's singular vision of fashion. He favors an inventive and unusual use of fabric and color, often pairing the unexpected to create cleanly cut designs that reveal the body. He revels in the female form, and in this silver panne velvet "Mercury" evening dress from his Fall/Winter 1994–95 collection, the fabric spills over the contours like liquid silver, while Beene's signature side cutouts and bare back expose and glorify the body.

List of Works Illustrated

Information is provided only for those materials that serve a largely decorative function.
Where not specifically noted, shoes, hats, and other accessories are in the style of the period.

HAUTE COUTURE (pp. 6–7)

TWO-PIECE EVENING DRESS
c. 1870
Designed by Charles Frederick Worth
English, active France, 1825–1895
Made by Worth & Bobergh, Paris (1857–1870)
Silk satin with tulle and lace
Gift of the heirs of Charlotte Hope Binney Tyler
Montgomery
1996-19-5b, c

FAN
Mid-19th century
Made in France
Painted parchment on mother-of-pearl sticks and
guards with silver gilt and a silk and metallic tassel
Gift of Mrs. William Carter Dickerman
1955-49-2

ARBITER OF STYLE (pp. 8–9)

TWO-PIECE DRESS
c. 1875
Designed by Charles Frederick Worth
Silk faille, satin, and velvet, with pleated organza,
machine-made appliqué, and fringe
Gift of the heirs of Charlotte Hope Binney Tyler
Montgomery
1996-19-6a, c

PARIS À LA MODE (pp. 10–11)

TWO-PIECE DAY DRESS
c. 1876
Designed by Emile Pingat
French, active 1860–96
Silk faille and striped silk faille and satin, with
machine-embroidered net, pleated organza, and
fringe
Gift of Mr. and Mrs. Ogden Wilkinson Headington in
memory of Ogden D. Wilkinson
1938-18-12a, b

HANDBAG
Early 20th century
Made in the United States
Crocheted rayon with beads
Gift of Dr. Mildred W. S. Schram
1953-45-14

Fashions for the theater and the ball
From *Revue de la Mode*, 1876
Musée de la Mode et du Costume, Paris
(© Photothèque des Musées de la Ville de Paris)

EXPORT WEAR (pp. 12–13)

TWO-PIECE EVENING DRESS
c. 1886–87
Designed by Charles Frederick Worth
Silk satin, faille, and brocade, with lace and
rhinestones
Gift of Mr. and Mrs. Owen Biddle
1978-2-1a, b

FAN
Late 19th century
Made in the United States
Painted paper over silk on mother-of-pearl sticks and
guards with inlaid abalone and gilding
Gift of Mrs. Pierre Fraley
1975-99-21

THE CULT OF CHIFFON (pp. 14–15)

TEA GOWN
c. 1905
Designed by Jeanne Hallée
French, active early 20th century
Silk chiffon over silk satin, with lace, ribbons, ribbon flowers, and fly fringe
Gift of Mrs. Priscilla de Mauduit
1967-16-2a, b

NEW YORK FINERY (pp. 16–17)

EVENING GOWN
c. 1907
Designed by Mrs. Dunstan
American, active 1891–1913
Silk satin with tulle, lace, tulle appliqué, rhinestones, sequins, and floss silk, chenille, and metallic thread embroidery
Gift of Mrs. Priscilla de Mauduit
1967-16-5a, b

FAN
Late 19th–early 20th century
Made in France
Bobbin lace and painted silk on ivory sticks and mother-of-pearl guards, with metal, rhinestones, and silk tassels
Gift of Mrs. Thomas Lynch Montgomery
1929-149-7

REFORMING FASHION (pp. 18–19)

WINTER WALKING OUTFIT
c. 1905
Made by Furst, Brussels
Fulled wool with silk appliqué, braid, embroidery, and silk-wrapped buttons
Gift of Mrs. George S. G. Cavendish, Mrs. Boyd Lee Spahr, Jr., Charles S. Wurts, and John W. Wurts
1955-29-15a, b

UMBRELLA
Early 20th century
Made by Stern Brothers, New York
Silk satin with faggoting on a metal frame with a wood handle and an engraved silver knob
Promised gift of Mrs. Frank Elliot

ELEGANT EMPORIUMS (pp. 20–21)

Left:
TWO-PIECE DRESS
c. 1904
Made by Gimbel Brothers, Philadelphia
Fulled wool and machine-made lace, with chiffon and machine top-stitching
Gift of an anonymous donor
1964-123-14a, b

PARASOL
c. 1902
Made in the United States
Lace over silk taffeta and sheer cotton on a metal and bamboo frame with an imitation tortoiseshell and engraved metal handle
Gift of Mrs. Joseph N. Snellenburg
1947-85-6

Right:
DINNER DRESS
c. 1912
Made by B. Altman Co., New York (est. 1865)
Silk chiffon and satin, with lace, tulle, bead and sequin embroidery, bead fringe, and silk flowers
Gift of Ms. Ann Pakradooni
1974-182-1

Florine Stettheimer
American, 1871–1948
Spring Sale at Bendel's
1921
Oil on canvas, 50 x 40" (127 x 101.6 cm)
Gift of Miss Ettie Stettheimer
1951-27-1

DREAM DRESSES (pp. 22–23)

"Happiness" Dinner Dress
Fall 1916
Designed by Lucile (Lady Duff Gordon)
English, active France and the United States, 1862–1935
Silk taffeta, satin, tulle, and chiffon, with lace, lace
appliqué and inset, ribbons, and silk flowers
Gift of Mrs. William H. Greene
1962-190-1

"Happiness" dinner dress designed by Lucile, Fall 1916
From a photographic album of Lucile designs
Special Collections, Fashion Institute of Technology,
New York

PORTRAIT OF FASHION (pp. 24–25)

Dress
c. 1921
Designed by Harry Collins
American, active early 20th century
Silk georgette and figured lamé, with lace, silk satin,
metallic thread embroidery, and silk and bead flowers
Gift of Mr. and Mrs. Anthony N. B. Garvan
1987-92-2

Philip A. de László
English, born Hungary, 1869–1937
*Portrait of Mrs. Francis P. Garvan and Her Four
Children*
1921
Oil on canvas, 110 x 88" (279.4 x 223.5 cm)
Gift of Mrs. Francis P. Garvan
1965-208-1

EGYPTOMANIA (pp. 26–27)

Left:
Dress and Hat
1923
Designed by Paul Poiret
French, 1879–1944
Dress: silk *crêpe de chine* and velvet, with silk and
metallic thread embroidery; hat: silk with leather
appliqué and metallic thread embroidery
Gift of Vera White
1951-126-3a, b

Shoes
c. 1929
Designed by Fenton Footwear for Saks Fifth Avenue,
New York (est. 1924)
Leather with enameled metal buckles
Gift of Mrs. Joseph N. Epstein
1959-136-1

Right:
Dress and Jacket
1923
Designed by Gustave Beer
French, born Germany, active 1905–29
Wool faille with silk embroidery, beading, and
painted metal medallions
Gift of Mrs. George S. G. Cavendish
1952-55-5a, b

Hat
1923
Made by Modes Andrée, Paris
Straw with silk ribbon and flowers
Gift of Mrs. George S. G. Cavendish
1952-55-5c

RENAISSANCE ROMANCE (pp. 28–29)

Wedding Ensemble
1925
Designed by Jeanne Lanvin
French, 1867–1946
Dress: silk georgette and tulle, with silver lamé
appliqué and silk and metallic thread embroidery;
underdress: silk satin with metallic lace; headdress:
silver lamé with wax orange blossoms
Gift of Mrs. William H. Lyon
1968-142-1a–c

Wedding dress designed by Jeanne Lanvin
From *La Gazette du Bon Ton,* 1921

THE PHILADELPHIA SEASON (pp. 30–31)

Left:
"La Belle Rose" Dress
1927
Designed by Madame Meeley
American, active 1920s
Silk tulle and satin, with lace, velvet ribbons, and silk flowers
Gift of Elizabeth S. Stetson Allen
1996-9-26

Right:
"La Belle Rose" Dress
1927
Designed by Madame Meeley
Silk tulle and satin, with lace, velvet ribbons, and silk flowers
Gift of Elizabeth S. Stetson Allen
1996-9-28

Photograph of Ann Stetson at her coming-out party, 1927
Department of Costume and Textiles, Philadelphia Museum of Art

IN FULL BLOOM (pp. 32–33)

Left:
Dress and Sash
c. 1923–25
Made in the United States
Silk chiffon with bead embroidery
Gift of an anonymous donor
1964-123-28a, b

Hat
1920s
Made by Ruby, Philadelphia and New York
Horsehair with coated cotton appliqué, embroidery, and beads
Gift of Mimi Favre
1993-86-1

Parasol
c. 1925–30
Probably made in France
Silk tabby with printed cotton appliqué on a metal frame with bone tips and a painted wood handle
Gift of Miss Ann E. Pester
1980-112-1

Right:
Dress and Sash
c. 1928–30
Made in the United States
Printed silk chiffon with a velvet ribbon sash
Gift of an anonymous donor
1964-81-23a, b

Hat
c. 1925–30
Made in the United States
Horsehair lace with velvet ribbon
Gift of Miss Percylee M. Hart
1973-227-48

Shoes
c. 1925
Made by Steigerwalt, Philadelphia
Silk and leather with metal and rhinestone buckles
Gift of Miss Margaretta S. Hinchman
1953-113-3a, b

PAST INTO PRESENT (pp. 34–35)

Left:
Long Gown
c. 1930
Designed by Mariano Fortuny y Madrazo
Spanish, active Italy, 1871–1949
Silk velvet stenciled with metallic pigment, with pleated silk, silk cord, and glass beads
Gift of Mrs. Thomas Raeburn White
1979-86-1

Right:
"Delphos" Gown
c. 1925
Designed by Mariano Fortuny y Madrazo
Pleated silk and glass beads
Gift of Mr. and Mrs. Fenton Keyes
1984-127-3a

Three-Quarter-Length Evening Coat
1929
Designed by Mariano Fortuny y Madrazo
Silk velvet stenciled with metallic pigment, with stenciled silk, silk cord, and glass beads
Gift of Mrs. Henry Clifford
1972-44-2

STREAMLINING STYLE (pp. 36–37)

EVENING GOWN
c. 1933
Designed by Augustabernard (Augusta Bernard)
French, 1886–1946
Imported by Thurn, New York and Paris
Silk satin and velvet
Gift of Mrs. Carroll S. Tyson
1957-33-3

Evening gown designed by Augustabernard, c. 1933
Photograph by George Hoyningen-Huene
From *Vogue*, 1933
Special Collections, Fashion Institute of Technology, New York

SHOCKING (pp. 38–39)

Left:
EVENING JACKET
Winter 1937–38
Designed by Elsa Schiaparelli
French, born Italy, 1890–1973
Wool twill with metallic strip and metal bead embroidery and metal buttons
Gift of Mme Elsa Schiaparelli
1969-232-9

Center:
EVENING JACKET
Winter 1937–38
Designed by Elsa Schiaparelli

Wool twill and silk velvet, with silk embroidery and rhinestone buttons
Gift of Mme Elsa Schiaparelli
1969-232-14

Right:
EVENING JACKET
Winter 1937–38
Designed by Elsa Schiaparelli
Silk velvet with silk and metallic thread embroidery, sequins, rhinestones, and metal buttons
Gift of Mme Elsa Schiaparelli
1969-232-19

BACK TO BUSTLES (pp. 40–41)

TWO-PIECE EVENING DRESS
Summer 1939
Designed by Elsa Schiaparelli
Striped silk satin and faille
Gift of Mme Elsa Schiaparelli
1969-232-29a, b

GLOVES
c. 1938
Designed by Elsa Schiaparelli
Silk shantung
Gift of Mme Elsa Schiaparelli
1969-232-59b, c

SHOES
c. 1935
Made by Steigerwalt, Philadelphia
Leather suede with snakeskin
Gift of an anonymous donor
1964-81-72a, b

Two-piece evening dress designed by Elsa Schiaparelli, 1939
Sketch by Christian Bérard
From *Vogue*, 1939
Philadelphia Museum of Art Library

HOLLYWOOD CLASSICS (pp. 42–43)

Left:
SUIT
c. 1947
Designed by Irene (Irene Lentz Gibbons)
American, 1901–1962
Designed for Nan Duskin, Philadelphia
Wool twill
Gift of an anonymous donor
1967-128-1a, b

Right:
SUIT
1947
Designed by Adrian (Gilbert Adrian Greenburgh, also called Gilbert Adrian)
American, 1903–1959
Wool twill
Gift of Adrian
1947-67-1a, b

Publicity photograph of Joan Crawford wearing a suit designed by Irene, c. 1942–45
(From *Star Style* by Patty Fox [Angel City Press])

SCULPTED IN SATIN (pp. 44–45)

Left:
EVENING GOWN
c. 1948
Designed by Charles James
American, born England, 1906–1978
Silk satin
Gift of Julia B. Leisenring
1995-88-1

Right:
EVENING GOWN
c. 1948
Designed by Charles James
Silk satin
Gift of Julia B. Leisenring
1995-88-2

Evening gowns designed by Charles James, 1940s
Photograph by Cecil Beaton, 1948
(Courtesy Sotheby's London)

DIOR BY DAY (pp. 46–47)

Left:
"AVENUE HOCHE" SUIT
Spring/Summer 1949
Designed by Christian Dior
French, 1905–1957
Wool twill with plastic buttons
Gift of Mrs. James D. Platt
1972-120-16a, b

"Avenue Hoche" suit designed by Christian Dior,
Spring/Summer 1949
Photograph by Willy Maywald
(© Assoc. Willy Maywald–ADAGP)

Right:
TWO-PIECE DRESS
Fall 1952
Designed by Christian Dior
Wool and silk twill with plastic buttons
Gift of Mrs. James D. Platt
1972-120-24a, b

HAT
c. 1952
Designed by Pauline Herman
American, active mid-20th century
Silk satin over buckram
Gift of Mrs. Franklin Levin
1974-7-14

PRESENTED AT COURT (pp. 48–49)

COURT PRESENTATION ENSEMBLE
1950
Designed by Norman Hartnell
English, 1901–1979
Dress: silk tulle and gold lamé, with silver lamé
appliqué, sequins, rhinestones, beads, and metallic
thread embroidery; train: silver lamé lined with gold
lamé and edged with tulle; headdress: ostrich feathers
and tulle on an imitation tortoiseshell comb
Gift of Gimbel Brothers, Philadelphia
1950-130-1a–c

COURT PRESENTATION FAN
c. 1934
Possibly made in France
Ostrich feathers on plastic sticks and guards with
rhinestones
Gift of Mrs. Randal Morgan
1950-87-2i

THE ESSENCE OF SPAIN (pp. 50–51)

EVENING DRESS WITH OVERDRESS
Spring 1951
Designed by Cristóbal Balenciaga
Spanish, active Spain and France, 1895–1972
Dress: silk organza; overdress: cotton piqué; skirt
support: glazed cotton with metal and feather boning;
petticoat: silk taffeta
Gift of John Wanamaker, Philadelphia
1951-73-1a–d

CASUALLY CHIC (pp. 52–53)

Left:
RESORT ENSEMBLE
Fall/Winter 1955–56
Designed by Emilio Pucci
Italian, 1914–1992
Printed cotton
Gift of Miss Lauren Bacall
1970-207-2a–c

Right:
BATHING DRESS
1953
Designed by Claire McCardell
American, 1905–1958
Wool knit with metal hook-and-eye closures
Gift of Miss Rubye Graham
1969-54-11

A MEASURE OF PERFECTION (pp. 54–55)

EVENING DRESS
1957
Designed by James Galanos
American, born 1924
Bead and sequin embroidery on sheer cotton
Gift of James Galanos
1957-103-1

THE TOTAL LOOK (pp. 56–57)

DAY ENSEMBLE
Fall 1964
Designed by Rudi Gernreich
American, born Austria, 1922–1985
Designed for Harmon Knitwear, Marinette,
Wisconsin
Wool knit
Gift of Mrs. Jack M. Friedland
1971-67-9a–d

HARDWEAR AND SOFTWEAR (pp. 58–59)

Left:
DRESS
1966
Designed by Paco Rabanne
French, born Spain, born 1934
Rhodoid plastic and metal
Gift of Miss Rubye Graham
1969-54-5

Right:
EVENING DRESS
c. 1973
Designed by Halston (Roy Halston Frowick)
American, 1932–1990
Nylon knit
Gift of the Arons Family Foundation in memory of
Edna S. Beron
1996-2-14

EVENING SANDALS
1980s
Made by Salvatore Ferragamo, Florence (est. 1929)
Leather
Gift of Mrs. Louis C. Madeira
1991-123-1a, b

EARRINGS
1970
Designed by Kenneth Jay Lane
American, born 1932
Gold plate with satin finish
Collection of the designer

THE MASTER'S TOUCH (pp. 60–61)

AFTERNOON DRESS AND JACKET
1968
Designed by Norman Norell (Norman David
Levinson)
American, 1900–1972
Silk taffeta and wool twill, with patent leather belt
and plastic buttons
Gift of Mrs. William Wolgin
1989-95-1a, b

FANTASY AND FASHION (pp. 62–63)

TWO-PIECE EVENING DRESS
1979
Designed by Zandra Rhodes
English, born 1940
Made for Nan Duskin, Philadelphia
Top and skirt: printed silk organza with acetate satin,
cording, and beads; underskirt: net over acetate satin
Gift of Mr. and Mrs. J. Welles Henderson
1994-90-9a–c

DAY INTO NIGHT (pp. 64–65)

SHORT EVENING DRESS
1986
Designed by Bill Blass
American, born 1922
Wool houndstooth plaid
Gift of Bill Blass
1997-13-5

Bill Blass
Sketch of short evening dress, 1997
Pen on paper
Department of Costume and Textiles, Philadelphia
Museum of Art

ARCHITECT OF FASHION (pp. 66–67)

SHORT EVENING DRESS
1987
Designed by Pierre Cardin
French, born Italy, born 1922
Silk taffeta with silk organza flower
Promised gift of Mrs. Martin Field

HEARTS AND FLOWERS (pp. 68–69)

SHORT EVENING DRESS
Spring/Summer 1988
Designed by Christian Lacroix
French, born 1951
Printed cotton cloqué with polyester ribbon and silk
flowers
Promised gift of Mrs. Martin Field

CONCEPT CLOTHES (pp. 70–71)

"Flying Saucer" Dress
Spring/Summer 1994
Designed by Issey Miyake
Japanese, born 1938
Heat-set polyester
Gift of Issey Miyake

REVEALING FORMS (pp. 72–73)

"Mercury" Evening Dress
Fall/Winter 1994–95
Designed by Geoffrey Beene
American, born 1927
Silver panne velvet
Gift of Geoffrey Beene

SHOES (pp. 78–79, clockwise from lower left)

Black Pump with Rhinestone Toe
c. 1980
Made by Delman, New York and Paris
Silk satin over leather with rhinestones
Promised gift of Cecile Lavine

Multicolored Mule
1970s
Made by Christian Dior, Paris (est. 1946)
Brocaded ribbon and metallic leather
Gift of Mrs. Louis C. Madeira
1991-123-2a

Pink Striped Short Boot
c. 1938
Designed by Elsa Schiaparelli
French, born Italy, 1890–1973
Made by Perugia for Padova, Paris
Silk satin over leather, with mother-of-pearl buttons
Gift of Mme Elsa Schiaparelli
1969-232-57a

Embroidered Lace Sandal
c. 1960
Made by Salvatore Ferragamo, Florence (est. 1929)
Embroidered and beaded lace with rhinestones,
leather, and gilt leather
Gift of Mrs. Howard H. Lewis
1979-43-11a

Black Diamond Sandal
c. 1939
Designed by Fenton Footwear for Saks Fifth Avenue,
New York (est. 1924)
Rayon velvet and silk satin over leather, with metallic
leather and a metal buckle with rhinestones
Gift of Mrs. John Price Jones
1976-22-10a

Pink and Black Pump
1952
Made by Pandora Footwear
Silk satin with machine embroidery over leather
Gift of Mrs. Joseph N. Epstein
1962-143-2a

White Satin Wedding Slipper
1874
Made by Maison Lapaque-Hoffman, Paris
Silk satin over leather, with a mother-of-pearl buckle
Gift of Mrs. George Stuart Patterson
1962-89-1b

Ivory Pump with Rhinestone Heel
c. 1923
Made by Frank Brothers, New York
Silk satin over leather, with a metal heel and buckle
with inset rhinestones
Gift of Mrs. George Edward Robinette
1964-72-3a

Navy Platform Sandal
c. 1943
Made by Saks Fifth Avenue, New York
Rayon velvet and satin over leather, with metallic
thread embroidery and metal studs
Gift of Mrs. Russell Richardson
1973-160-1b

Needlepoint Slipper
Mid-19th century
Made by R. Smith and Co., Philadelphia
Wool cross-stitch on canvas over leather, with a silk
tassel
Gift of Mrs. W. Logan MacCoy
1955-78-11b

SATIN AND BROCADE PUMP WITH RHINESTONE HEEL
1918–23
Made in the United States
Silk satin and metallic brocade over leather, with
ribbon, chiffon, metallic lace, and rhinestones, and a
metallic lacquered heel with inset rhinestones
Gift of Mrs. George Edward Robinette
1964-72-2a

RED VELVET SANDAL
1950
Made by Waldo, J. N. Claflin, Philadelphia
Rayon velvet and satin over leather, with elastic and
rhinestones
Gift of Miss Beatrice Wolfe
1959-125-1b

METALLIC PUMP WITH FLOWERS
c. 1929
Made by Gimbel Brothers, Philadelphia
Gilt and silver leather with painted flowers
Gift of Walter White Buckley
1954-43-13b

GOLD LAMÉ BOOT
Early 20th century
Made by Strawbridge and Clothier, Philadelphia
Gold lamé over leather, with metal beads and buttons
Gift of Mrs. Richard Greenwood
1956-106-47b

HATS (pp. 84–85, clockwise from lower left)

DOMED STRAW HAT
1966
Designed by Gustave Tassell
American, born 1926
Straw braid
Gift of Gustave Tassell
1973-33-44

MULTICOLORED PETAL HAT
1951
Designed by Cesare Canessa
Italian, active mid-20th century
Painted cotton velveteen petals on rayon knit over
buckram
Gift of Mrs. John Wintersteen
1960-141-2

ORANGE VELVET HAT
c. 1917–20
Made by Joseph G. Darlington and Co., Philadelphia
(est. 1878)
Silk velvet over buckram, with silk moiré faille
Gift of the Misses Constance A. and Adelaide S. Jones
1972-178-16

STRAW HAT WITH PINECONES
c. 1958
Designed by Lilly Daché
American, born France, 1907–1990
Braided and laminated straw decoration over straw
braid with net
Gift of Mrs. Henry Clifford
1972-44-10

YELLOW EMBROIDERED STRAW HAT
c. 1923
Made by Warshauer, Paris and New York
Sold through Livingston Brothers, San Francisco
Straw braid with silk georgette and bead embroidery
Gift of Mrs. Francis John Rumpf
1972-189-35

PLUSH HAT WITH ROSES
c. 1908
Made by Joseph G. Darlington and Co., Philadelphia
Silk plush with silk velvet and artificial flowers
Gift of an anonymous donor
1964-123-70

STRAW HAT WITH LACE
1910
Designed by Mme Georgette
French, early 20th century
Straw braid with lace, velvet ribbon, and silk roses
Gift of Marie Josephine Rozet and Rebecca
Mandeville Rozet Hunt
1935-13-86

PINK WAVE HAT
1988
Designed by Hubert de Givenchy
French, born 1927
Silk satin over buckram with silk velvet
Purchased with funds contributed by an anonymous
donor
1993-52-3

BLACK LACE HAT
c. 1910
Designed by Mme Georgette
Lace over wire frame with silk roses
Gift of Mrs. Pierre Fraley
1994-108-1

"MONDRIAN" HAT
c. 1965
Designed by Sally Victor
American, c. 1894–1977
Wool felt with ribbon
Gift of Miss Rubye Graham
1966-35-2

HAT WITH OSTRICH PLUMES
c. 1910
Made by Guillard Soeurs, Paris
Straw with lace, silk roses, and ostrich feathers
Gift of Mrs. Pierre Fraley
1975-99-17